EVANGELISTIC
SERMON OUTLINES

Billy Apostolon

BAKER BOOK HOUSE
Grand Rapids, Michigan

Formerly published under the title
The Voice of Evangelism

ISBN: 0-8010-0144-7

Fourteenth printing, January 1999

Printed in the United States of America

For information about academic books, resources for
Christian leaders, and all new releases available from
Baker Book House, visit our web site:
http://www.bakerbooks.com/

FOREWORD

Before our Lord Jesus Christ ascended into Heaven to be on the right hand of God the Father, He spoke to believers and revealed to them that it was His plan for them to be, "The Voice of Evangelism" in the beginning of the Dispensation of Grace, when he said: "All power is given unto me in Heaven and in earth" (Matt. 28:18); "Ye shall receive power after that the Holy Ghost is come upon you: and ye shall be witnesses unto me both in Jerusalem, and in all Judaea, and in Samaria, and unto the uttermost part of the earth" (Acts 1:8); "Go ye therefore, and teach all nations, baptizing them in the name of the Father, and of the Son, and of the Holy Ghost: Teaching them to observe all things whatsoever I have commanded you: and, lo I am with you alway, even unto the end of the world" (Matt. 28:19, 20).

The Apostle Paul, that noble servant of the Lord, revealed that the purpose of his life was to be used as, "The Voice of Evangelism" in the spread of the gospel into the uttermost parts of the world when he said: "I am a debtor both to the Greeks, and to the Barbarians; both to the wise, and to the unwise" (Rom. 1:14); "I am set for the defense of the gospel" (Phil. 1:17); "For I am not ashamed of the gospel of Christ; for it is the power of God unto salvation to every one that believeth" (Rom. 1:16); "For necessity is laid upon me; yea, woe is unto me, if I preach not the gospel" (I Cor. 9:16).

We wish to express our heartfelt appreciation to the Lord's servants who by their love to the Lord Jesus have made consecrated contributions which have made this work possible.

It is our prayer as we commit "The Voice of Evangelism" into the hands of our Lord Jesus, that the Holy Spirit may use this work through dedicated servants to glorify the Name that is above every name by leading those who are now in the kingdom of darkness into the Kingdom of God's Dear Son, and to bring those who are now carnal Christians to a place where they will render a consecrated service to our Matchless Redeemer.

— Billy Apostolon

Hinton, West Virginia

DEDICATION

This book is dedicated to my former pastor
CHARLES HEBER MARTIN
former pastor of the
BELLEPOINT BAPTIST CHURCH
who by his godly life, devotion to our
LORD JESUS CHRIST
and earnest desire to see souls won to Christ has been
THE VOICE OF EVANGELISM
in our area for as long as I can remember.

CONTENTS

THE VOICE OF EVANGELISM (1)
ISAIAH 58:1

I. THE VOICE OF EVANGELISM DURING THE TIME PRE-CEDING THE FLOOD WAS NOAH.
1. Noah lived during a time of great wickedness; Gen. 6:5.
2. Noah was warned by God about the judgment of the flood; Heb. 11:7.
3. Noah, the preacher of righteousness, built an ark as a means of deliverance from the flood; II Peter 2:5; Gen. 6:14-22.

II. THE VOICE OF EVANGELISM DURING THE EXODUS AND WILDERNESS JOURNEY WAS MOSES.
1. Moses was called and commissioned by the Lord; Exod. 3:3, 4, 10.
2. Moses led Israel out of Egypt on the basis of the shed blood that was applied on the two side posts and the upper door posts of the houses; Exod. 12:7, 13.

III. THE VOICE OF EVANGELISM DURING THE TIME OF THE JUDGES WAS SAMSON.
1. Samson had a miraculous birth; Judg. 13:3, 22-24.
2. Samson was moved by the Spirit of the Lord; Judg. 13:25.
3. Samson was a deliverer of Israel from the hands of the Philistines; Judg. 13:5; 14:9; 15:13-17; 16:21-31.

IV. THE VOICE OF EVANGELISM TO NINEVEH WAS JONAH.
1. Jonah was a prophet of Israel whom God sent to warn the Nine-vites of their wickedness; Jonah 1:2.
2. Jonah was disobedient to the Lord's call, was punished, later re-pented and was recommissioned to preach to Nineveh; Jonah 1:3-17; 2; 3:1, 2.
3. Jonah was used to bring the Ninevites to repentance; Jonah 3:3-10.

V. THE VOICE OF EVANGELISM TO THE TEN TRIBES OF IS-RAEL WAS AMOS.
1. Amos was a God chosen preacher; Amos 7:14, 15.
2. Amos warned the ten tribes to, "Prepare To Meet God."; Amos 4:12.

VI. THE VOICE OF EVANGELISM TO THE TRIBE OF JUDAH WAS ISAIAH.
1. Isaiah revealed the sinfulness of Judah; Isa. 1:4-9.
2. Isaiah revealed the blessings which would come through the com-ing Saviour; Isa. 7:14; 9:6, 7.

VII. THE VOICE OF EVANGELISM DURING ISRAEL AND JU-DAH'S EXILE WAS THE PROPHET DANIEL.
1. Daniel revealed God's coming judgment upon Belshazzar's king-dom; Dan. 5:17-28.
2. Daniel served God in the midst of persecution; Dan. 6:7-23.

           — Billy Apostolon

THE VOICE OF EVANGELISM (2)
EZEKIEL 33:7-11

I. THE VOICE OF EVANGELISM IMMEDIATELY PRECEDING OUR LORD'S PUBLIC MINISTRY WAS JOHN THE BAPTIST.
   1. John the Baptist came to bear witness that men might believe in Christ; John 1:7, 8.
   2. John the Baptist rebuked sin and preached repentance; Matt. 3:7, 8; 14:4; Mark 6:18; Luke 3:18, 19.

II. THE VOICE OF EVANGELISM DURING OUR LORD'S EARTHLY MINISTRY WAS THE LORD JESUS HIMSELF.
   1. Our Lord came to call sinners to repentance; Luke 5:32; 13:3, 5; Matt. 4:17.
   2. Our Lord invited the sinful multitudes to come to Him for rest; Matt. 11:28-30.

III. THE VOICE OF EVANGELISM ON THE DAY OF PENTECOST WAS THE APOSTLE PETER.
   1. Peter preached Christ; Acts 2:22-24, 32.
   2. Peter preached in the convicting power of the Holy Spirit; Acts 2:37, 38.

IV. THE VOICE OF EVANGELISM TO ISRAEL CONCERNING THEIR UNBELIEF WAS STEPHEN, THE FIRST CHRISTIAN MARTYR.
   1. Stephen was full of faith and the Holy Spirit; Acts 6:5, 8.
   2. Stephen preached with irresistible wisdom and condemned Israel for their unbelief; Acts 6:10; 7:51.

V. THE VOICE OF EVANGELISM WHEN THE GOSPEL WAS BEING SPREAD INTO SAMARIA WAS THE DEACON PHILIP.
   1. Philip preached Christ in such a manner that the multitude gave heed to his message; Acts 8:5, 6.
   2. Philip saw the result of preaching a Christ honoring gospel; Acts 8:7, 8, 12.

VI. THE VOICE OF EVANGELISM DURING THE SPREAD OF THE GOSPEL INTO THE UTTERMOST PARTS OF THE WORLD WAS THE APOSTLE PAUL.
   1. Paul preached in the synagogue at Athens, that justification was by faith in Jesus Christ; Acts 13:38, 39.
   2. Paul preached on Mar's Hill, that God will judge the world by Jesus Christ; Acts 17:30, 31.

VII. THE VOICE OF EVANGELISM DURING THIS PRESENT AGE OF GRACE IS ALL NEW TESTAMENT PREACHERS.
   1. New Testament preachers are ambassadors for Christ; II Cor. 5:20.
   2. New Testament preachers are to seek the salvation of the lost; I Cor. 10:33.

— Billy Apostolon

THE CHRISTIAN PUTTING FIRST THINGS FIRST
MATTHEW 6:33

INTRODUCTION: There are some Christians who are unconcerned about the things of the Lord. There are other Christians who seek to put the Lord first in this life. It is our desire in this message to mention some of the things that should have first place in the Christian's life.

I. THE FIRST AMONG THE CHRISTIAN'S COMPANIONS SHOULD BE THE LORD JESUS CHRIST.
   1. Because Jesus is a Companion who has given His life for us; Rom. 5:8; John 10:11, 15.
   2. Because Jesus is a Companion who is closer than a brother; Prov. 18:24.
   3. Because Jesus is a Companion who knows all of our needs; John 2:25; I Peter 5:7.
   4. Because Jesus is a Companion who gives us victory for Christian living; I Cor. 15:57; I John 5:4.

II. THE FIRST AMONG THE CHRISTIAN'S BOOKS SHOULD BE THE BIBLE.
   1. Because the Bible is the most precious Book in the world; Ps. 19:10.
   2. Because the Bible is the all sufficient Book; Luke 16:29, 31.
   3. Because the Bible was written for our instructions; Rom. 15:4.
   4. Because the Bible is able to cleanse the Christian's path; Ps. 119:9.

III. THE FIRST PART OF THE CHRISTIAN'S EARNINGS SHOULD BE THE TITHE.
   1. Because the Lord Jesus taught tithing; Luke 11:42.
   2. Because the Apostle Paul emphasized tithing; I Cor. 16:2; II Cor. 9:6-8.
   3. Because the tithe is a return to God for His blessings; Gen. 28:22.
   4. Because by tithing Christians will receive a blessing in this life; Mal. 3:10.

IV. THE FIRST AMONG INSTITUTIONS HONORED BY THE CHRISTIAN SHOULD BE THE CHURCH.
   1. Because the Church has been purchased by the Blood of Christ; Acts 20:28.
   2. Because the Lord Jesus is the Chief Corner Stone of the Church; Eph. 2:19, 20.
   3. Because the Church is loved by the Lord Jesus Christ; Eph. 5:25.
   4. Because the Church is being cleansed by Christ; I Cor. 6:11.

V. THE FIRST AMONG THE CHRISTIAN'S ENTERPRISES SHOULD BE SOUL-WINNING.
   1. Because our Lord Jesus has commanded that Christians witness for Him; Matt. 28:18-20; Acts 1:8.
   2. Because the power of the Holy Spirit is available to those who witness; Luke 24:49.
   3. Because those who follow Jesus should be fishers of men; Matt. 4:19; Mark 1:17.
   4. Because the Christian's duty is to be an ambassador for Christ; II Cor. 5:20.

— Billy Apostolon

STEADFAST UNMOVEABLE SAINTS
I CORINTHIANS 15:58

INTRODUCTION: Today, many professing Christians are growing so lukewarm that it is practically impossible to tell them from individuals who have not made a profession of faith. There is a great need, in our day, for Christians who will be faithful in their service to the Lord by being steadfast, unmoveable and always abounding in the work of the Lord. Let us consider from God's Word some characteristics of those who are "steadfast, unmoveable" Saints.

I. STEADFAST UNMOVEABLE SAINTS HAVE PEACE WITH GOD.
  1. Peace with God is something about which the unsaved individual knows nothing; Isa. 57:20, 21.
  2. Peace with God is through the merits of Christ's shed blood; Col. 1:20.
  3. Peace with God is the result of being justified by faith; Rom. 5:1.

II. STEADFAST UNMOVEABLE SAINTS FOLLOW JESUS.
  1. They follow Him because they know Him; II Tim. 1:12.
  2. They follow Him because they know His voice; John 10:4.
  3. They follow Him because they love Him; I Peter 1:8.

III. STEADFAST UNMOVEABLE SAINTS ABIDE IN CHRIST.
  1. They abide in Him in order to have a fruitful Christian life; John 15:5.
  2. They must abide in Him in order to be successful in prayer; John 15:7.
  3. They know that they abide in Him by the Holy Spirit's witness; I John 3:24.

IV. STEADFAST UNMOVEABLE SAINTS AVOID CHURCH DIVISIONS.
  1. Divisions are contrary to the desires of the Lord Jesus Christ; John 17:21-23.
  2. Divisions are the result of carnality; I Cor. 3:3.
  3. Divisions cause a weakness among God's people; Matt. 12:25.

V. STEADFAST UNMOVEABLE SAINTS KNOW HOW TO DEAL WITH TEMPTATIONS.
  1. They pray to be kept from temptations; Matt. 6:13; 26:41.
  2. They avoid the way of temptations; Prov. 4:14, 15; I Peter 5:8.
  3. They know that the Lord is able to deliver them from temptations; I Cor. 10:13.

VI. STEADFAST UNMOVEABLE SAINTS ARE NOT INFLUENCED BY FALSE TEACHERS.
  1. They know that false teachers speak things contrary to God's Word; Acts 20:30.
  2. They know that false teachers teach things that are destructive to their faith; II Tim. 2:18.
  3. They know that false teachers should be avoided; Jer. 23:16; 29:8.

— Billy Apostolon

DOES THE BIBLE HAVE THE ANSWER?

II TIMOTHY 3:15-17

INTRODUCTION: I have been asked by Christians, by those who are not Christians, and by students questions that often puzzle those who are journeying through this life. In answering these questions, I say, "What does the Bible say?" I use this means of meeting the questions that come to me because I believe that the Bible has the answer to the questions that are often difficult to answer. Let us turn to the Bible, today, and let the Bible answer some questions for us.

I. DOES THE BIBLE HAVE THE ANSWER CONCERNING GOD'S ATTRIBUTES?
1. The Bible states that God is omnipotent; Gen. 17:1; Matt. 19:26.
2. The Bible states that God is omnipresent; Ps. 139:7; Jer. 23:23, 24.
3. The Bible states that God is omniscient; Acts 15:18; I John 3:20.

II. DOES THE BIBLE HAVE THE ANSWER CONCERNING SATAN?
1. The Bible emphasizes that Satan is the author of man's fall; Gen. 3:1, 6, 14, 24.
2. That Satan is the God of the unregenerate world; II Cor. 4:4.
3. That Satan was defeated by Christ's death; Heb. 2:14; Col. 2:15.

III. DOES THE BIBLE HAVE THE ANSWER CONCERNING SIN?
1. The Bible declares that all unrighteousness is sin; I John 5:17.
2. The Bible declares that sin is universal; Rom. 5:12.
3. The Bible declares that the wages of sin is death; Rom. 6:23.

IV. DOES THE BIBLE HAVE THE ANSWER CONCERNING THE LORD JESUS CHRIST?
1. The Bible says that Jesus is the Son of God; Luke 1:35.
2. The Bible says that Jesus is the Revelation of God; John 1:18.
3. The Bible says that Jesus is the Way to the Father; John 14:6.

V. DOES THE BIBLE HAVE THE ANSWER CONCERNING SALVATION?
1. The Bible reveals that salvation is the deliverance from sin; Matt. 1:21; I John 3:5.
2. That salvation is not by man's works; II Tim. 1:9; Rom. 11:6.
3. That salvation is by personal faith in Jesus Christ; Acts 16:30, 31.

VI. DOES THE BIBLE HAVE THE ANSWER CONCERNING THE HOLY SPIRIT?
1. The Bible relates that the Holy Spirit convicts the unregenerate of sin; John 16:8-11.
2. That by the Holy Spirit the unregenerate are regenerated; John 3:6.
3. The Bible relates that the Holy Spirit directs the work of the Church; Acts 13:2; 16:6, 7; Eph. 2:22.

VII. DOES THE BIBLE HAVE THE ANSWER CONCERNING HEAVEN?
1. The Bible states that God made Heaven; Gen. 1:1; Rev. 10:6.
2. The Bible states what Heaven will be like; Rev. 21:1-4.
3. The Bible states that Heaven will be everlasting; Ps. 89:29; II Cor. 5:1

— Billy Apostolon

WHY EVERY HOME SHOULD HAVE A FAMILY ALTAR
DEUTERONOMY 6:3-7; 11:18, 19; PROVERBS 22:6

INTRODUCTION: Juvenile delinquency today is at an all time high. Young people accompanied by broken-hearted parents are appearing before courts of law throughout America. Because of this existing condition there is a greater need now than ever before for the establishment of the family altar in the home. The family altar is needed because:

I. IT IS A MEANS BY WHICH THE WORD OF GOD CAN BE EXALTED IN THE HOME.
   1. The Bible should be exalted because it was given by inspiration of God; II Tim. 3:16.
   2. The Bible should be exalted because it was written for our instruction; Rom. 15:4.
   3. The Bible should be exalted because it is an unerring guide; Prov. 6:23; II Peter 1:19.

II. IT IS A MEANS BY WHICH THE COMPLETE FAMILY CAN PRAY TOGETHER.
   1. Private prayer was commanded by our Lord Jesus Christ; Matt. 6:6.
   2. Private prayer was the constant practice of our Lord Jesus Christ; Matt. 14:23; Mark 1:35.
   3. Private prayer should be hindered by nothing; Dan. 6:6-10.

III. IT WILL SET AN EXAMPLE FOR OTHERS.
   1. We are living epistles before others; II Cor. 3:2.
   2. We should let our light shine before others; Matt. 5:16.
   3. We should let others know that we have a new life; Rom. 6:4.

IV. IT IS A MEANS BY WHICH CHILDREN CAN BE TAUGHT THEIR DUTY TO GOD.
   1. Children should be taught to remember God in youth; Eccles. 12:1.
   2. Children should be taught to fear God; Prov. 24:21.
   3. Children should be taught to obey God; Deut. 30:2.

V. IT IS A MEANS BY WHICH CHILDREN CAN BE TAUGHT THEIR DUTY TO THEIR PARENTS.
   1. Children should be taught to honor their parents; Exod. 20:12; Heb. 2:9.
   2. Children should be taught to heed parents' teachings; Prov. 1:8, 9.
   3. Children should be taught responsibility to parents; I Tim. 5:4.

VI. IT IS A MEANS BY WHICH CHILDREN CAN BE WON TO CHRIST.
   1. Children should be instructed in the ways of the Lord; Deut. 31:12, 13; Prov. 22:6.
   2. Children should be taught the way of salvation; John 3:16; Eph. 2:8, 9.
   3. Children should be brought to Christ; Mark 10:13-16.

VII. IT IS A MEANS BY WHICH CHRISTIANS CAN GROW IN GRACE.
   1. Christians need grace in order to serve the Lord; Heb. 12:28.
   2. Christians should seek to grow in grace; II Peter 3:18.
   3. Christians should seek to be strong in grace; II Tim. 2:1.

— Billy Apostolon

THE HORRORS OF HELL

MATTHEW 13:47-50

I. HELL WILL BE A HORROR BECAUSE OF ITS INHABITANTS.
1. The nations who forget God will be there; Ps. 9:17.
2. The wicked unregenerate Christ rejectors will be there; Rev. 21:8.
3. The abominable will be there; Rev. 21:7.
4. The angels who sinned will be there; II Peter 2:4.
5. The Devil, the beast, and the false prophet will be there; Rev. 19:10; 20:10.
6. The ones whose names are not in the Book 'of Life will be there; Matt. 25:41.

II. HELL WILL BE A HORROR BECAUSE OF THE TEMPERATURE THERE.
1. Hell will be a place of fire and brimstone; Rev. 19:20.
2. Hell will be filled with literal fire; Matt. 5:25; 18:9.
3. Hell will have fire that never shall be quenched; Mark 9:44.

III. HELL WILL BE A HORROR BECAUSE OF THE ACTIVITIES THERE.
1. There will be the gnashing of teeth in Hell; Matt. 13:42.
2. There will be shame and contempt in Hell; Dan. 12:2.
3. There will be a thirst that never shall be quenched; Luke 16:24, 25.
4. There will be an unsoothable sorrow in Hell; Ps. 18:5.
5. There will be no rest in Hell; Rev. 14:11.
6. There will be a continual torment in Hell; Rev. 20:10.

IV. HELL WILL BE A HORROR BECAUSE ONE WILL HAVE HIS MEMORY THERE.
1. There will be the memory of God's love; John 3:16.
2. There will be the memory of gospel sermons; Rom. 10:17.
3. There will be the memory of invitations to receive Christ which were rejected; Rev. 22:17.
4. There will be the memory of unsaved loved ones; Luke 16:27, 28.
5. There will be the memory that all hope is gone; John 8:21, 24.

V. HELL WILL BE A HORROR BECAUSE IT WILL BE FOREVER.
1. Hell has been enlarged to hold the multitude that will be there; Isa. 5:14.
2. Hell has no exits by which its inhabitants can escape; Luke 16:26.
3. Hell is everlasting in its duration; Matt. 25:46.

— Billy Apostolon

WHAT IS A CHRISTIAN?

ACTS 11:26

INTRODUCTION: It is not my purpose to talk to you about why they were called Christians, but I want, if I can, to try to tell you what, in the light of the New Testament, a Christian really is.

I. WHAT A CHRISTIAN IS AND IS NOT.
1. What a Christian is not.
   a. Living in a so-called Christian country does not make one a Christian.
   b. Being baptized, joining the church and taking communion does not make one a Christian.
   c. Having a Christian father and mother does not make one a Christian.
2. What a Christian is. In the light of the New Testament, a Christian is a person in whose life four things have taken place.
   a. First, conviction.
   b. Second, repentance.
   c. Third, conversion.
   d. Fourth, the New Birth.

II. WHY YOU SHOULD BE A CHRISTIAN.
1. You should become a Christian because it is right.
   a. God expects me to get the most possible out of life and I owe it to myself to treat myself square.
   b. The man who rejects Jesus Christ and lives in sin murders his immortal soul. He commits suicide for all eternity.
2. You owe it to your fellow man to become a Christian.
3. You owe it to Jesus Christ to become a Christian.
4. You should become a Christian because it is safe.
5. You should become a Christian because gratitude demands it.
6. You should become a Christian now, because of the uncertainty of life.
   a. It is always today with God. It is always tomorrow with the fool.
   b. There was never a bigger lie born in Hell, or hatched in the domain of the Devil, than the statement, "You have plenty of time"; II Cor. 6:2.

— Bob Jones, Sr.

14

WHAT SHALL I DO THEN WITH JESUS?

MATTHEW 27:11-16

I. THE QUESTION ANALYZED.
1. First, it is a personal question.
2. Second, the question requires action.
3. Third, the question is about Jesus Christ and about nothing else and nobody else under Heaven.

II. THE INESCAPABLE QUESTION YOU CANNOT DODGE.
1. Pilate tried to evade this question.
   a. He sent Jesus to Herod; Luke 23:6, 7.
   b. He found no cause of death in Christ; Luke 23:22.
   c. He tried a second time to avoid the decision about Christ; Luke 23:20, 21, 23, 24.
2. There are several reasons why no man can dodge this issue.
   a. Because Christ is the Creator; John 1:3.
   b. Because Christ sustains individuals; Ps. 139:7-12.
   c. Because Christ is the only Saviour; Acts 4:12.
   d. Because Christ will be the Judge; John 5:22, 27; Acts 10:42.

III. JESUS OR BARABBAS?
There are three heavy factors which every sinner must weigh when he faces Jesus Christ and decides what he shall do with Christ.
   a. First, there is Satan, a personal Devil.
   b. Second, there must be a decision on the sin question.
   c. Third, there must be the consideration of self.

IV. ALTERNATE CHOICES: WHAT YOU CAN DO WITH JESUS.
1. First, you must be for or against Him; Matt. 12:30; Luke 11:23.
2. Second, everyone must either love Him or hate Him; Matt. 6:24.
3. Third, you must either accept Him or reject Him; John 1:12; Rom. 6:23.
4. Fourth, you must crown Christ as Lord, or crucify Him.
   a. Christ is really the "prince of the kings of the earth"; Rev. 1:5.
   b. Those who reject Christ take part in His crucifixion; Heb. 6:4-6.
5. Fifth, you can confess Him or deny Him; Matt. 10:32, 33; Luke 9:26.

V. WHAT YOU DO WITH JESUS NOW SETTLES WHAT HE WILL DO WITH YOU LATER.
1. Eternal salvation depends altogether on the way you answer the question, "What shall I do then with Jesus?" I John 5:11, 12.
2. Now, the question is, What will you do with the pleading Jesus? but one day it will be, What will Jesus do with you? Rev. 20:15.

— Adapted from John R. Rice

GOD'S SCHEME OF SALVATION IS AS A GREAT HARBOR

HEBREWS 2:3

INTRODUCTION: After a wild night, we had gone down to the harbor, over whose arms the angry waves had been dashing with the boom of thunder while the winds were howling like the furies of the olden fables. Yet, the ships which had put in during the night were riding in safety, with the sailors resting or repairing torn places in the sails, unstirred by the storm which was raging without. Such a refuge or harbor is a fit emblem of salvation, where tempest-driven souls find shelter and peace.

I. IT IS GREAT IN ITS SWEEP.
1. There is sufficient room in it for navies of souls to ride at anchor.
2. There is within its sweep the capacity to embrace a ruined world.
3. There is space enough for every ship of Adam's race which has been launched from the shores of time; I John 2:2.

II. IT IS GREAT IN ITS FOUNDATION.
1. The chief requisite in constructing a sea-wall is to get a foundation down to the granite rock which can stand unmoved amid the heaviest seas.
2. God's harbor has a foundation mighty enough to inspire a strong consolation in those who have fled to it for refuge; Heb. 6:18, 19; I Cor. 3:11.

III. IT WAS GREAT IN ITS COST.
1. By the tubular bridge on the Menai Straits stands a column, which records the names of those who perished during the construction of that great triumph of engineering skill. Nothing is said of the money spent; only of the lives sacrificed.
2. By the harbor of our salvation rises a column with the inscription: Sacred to the memory of the Son of God, who gave His life as a sacrifice for the sin of the world; Rom. 5:8.

IV. IT HAS BEEN GREAT IN ITS ANNOUNCEMENT.
1. The announcement has been made by angels; Luke 2:9-14.
2. The announcement has been made by the Lord Jesus; Matt. 11:28-30; John 6:35, 37.
3. The announcement has been made by New Testament preachers; Acts 13:38, 39.
4. The announcement has been testified to by God the Father's omnipotent power; Acts 8:5-8.

— Adapted from F. B. Meyer in *The Biblical Illustrator*

CHRIST'S THREEFOLD MISSION
JOHN 10:1-18

INTRODUCTION: Every leaf of the Gospels contains precious treasures. These eighteen verses are no exception to such claims. Their truths are many and marvelous. I have elected to discuss of these truths, suggested by three statements of Jesus regarding Himself: (1) "I am the door"; (2) "I am come that they might have life, and that they might have it more abundantly"; and (3) "I am the good shepherd, the good shepherd giveth his life for the sheep." I want to discuss these three claims under three subjects; (1) The New Birth; (2) The Abundant Life; and (3) The Blessed Lordship.

I. THE NEW BIRTH.

1. Christ is the simple way to God; John 3:16.

2. Christ is the sole way to God; John 10:8, 9.

3. Christ is the satisfactory way to God; John 10:9.

II. THE ABUNDANT LIFE.

1. Christ alone is the Author of life; John 1:4.

2. Christ is the Arbiter of all grace; John 10:27, 28.

3. Christ dispenses abundant blessing; John 10:10.

III. THE BLESSED LORDSHIP.

1. This Lordship involves a personal relationship; John 10:11a. "I am the good shepherd."

2. This Lordship makes an abundant provision more abundant; Luke 11:3.

3. This Lordship assures adequate protection; John 10:11b. "The good shepherd giveth his life for the sheep."

CONCLUSION: With earthly shepherds, one might lose his life for the sheep, and yet the sheep perish; but not so with the Lord who is our Shepherd. When He gives His life for us, it is that ours might be saved. We are saved by His death, for in death He is with us and for us, and in death He is conquering our enemy.

— Adapted from W. B. Riley

JESUS THE CHRIST AS SIN-BEARER
GOD'S JUSTICE AND LOVE

JOHN 3:16; ROMANS 3:26; ISAIAH 53:5, 6; I CORINTHIANS 15:3; GALA-
TIANS 1:3, 4; 3:13; 2:20; I PETER 2:24; 3:18; MATTHEW 20:28; 26:28; I
TIMOTHY 2:5, 6; TITUS 2:13, 14; HEBREWS 10:10, 14; 9:12; REVELATION
5:9; I JOHN 4:10

I. IS CHRIST'S SUBSTITUTIONARY ATONEMENT MORALLY
   WRONG?
   1. Some occupying the highest positions in literary and theological
      institutions, say that it is morally wrong for the innocent to suffer
      the penalty of the guilty.
      a. In the first place it is not morally wrong, because God would
         not do anything morally wrong.
      b. It is not morally wrong, because God did let the innocent suf-
         fer the penalty of the guilty.

II. CHRIST'S DEATH IS THE ONLY RIGHTEOUS WAY GOD
    COULD SAVE SINNERS.
    Let us consider carefully what it really means when we are told that
    "Christ died for our sins"; I Cor. 15:3.
      a. That he "gave himself for our sins"; Gal. 1:4.
      b. That "his own self bare our sins in his own body on the tree";
         I Peter 2:24.
      c. That "Christ also suffered for sins once, the righteous for the
         unrighteous"; I Peter 3:18.
      d. "That he might himself be just and the justifier of him that
         hath faith in Jesus"; Rom. 3:26.

III. CHRIST'S SUFFERING PAID FOR ALL SINS OF THE BE-
     LIEVER.
     1. God the Father laid on Christ the iniquity of us all; Isa. 53:6.
     2. Christ died for all of the sins of the believer; Gal. 1:4.
     3. Christ gave Himself to redeem us from all iniquity; Titus 2:13, 14.
     4. Through Christ the believer is justified from all things; Acts 13:39.

IV. THE VICARIOUS ATONEMENT REQUIRES THE DEITY OF
    CHRIST.
      a. First, if He had not been Deity, God manifest in the flesh, His
         dying for our sins would not have been redemption but a mere
         makeshift; I Cor. 15:3; Heb. 10:4.
      b. Second, had the Saviour been anything other than God mani-
         fest in the flesh, He would have won men from God and
         alienated them from God.

V. THE AWFUL SIN OF REJECTING CHRIST'S ATONING
   DEATH.
   1. The greatest crime that is ever committed on this earth is to re-
      ject this "so great salvation"; Heb. 2:3.
   2. God has warned that, ". . . without shedding of blood is no remis-
      sion"; Heb. 9:22.   — Adapted from T. T. Martin

18

GIVING GOD OUR BEST
GENESIS 22:1-19

INTRODUCTION: Here is something most of us have never really tried; giving God our best! But that is precisely what God called upon Abraham to give, and what he calls upon each of us to give. Let us note the four great experiences which came to Abraham in this test through which God caused him to pass.

I. ABRAHAM'S TESTING CALL FROM GOD: UNMISTAKABLY GOD CALLED FOR ABRAHAM'S BEST JUST AS HE CALLS FOR OUR BEST.
   1. God calls for the best of our love; Matt. 22:35-40; Mark 12:28-34.
   2. God calls for the best of our gifts; Lev. 27:30-33; Matt. 6:19-33.
   3. God calls for the best of our labors; Matt. 19:27-30; 10:24-42.
   4. God calls for the best of our loyalty; Luke 9:21-26; 9:57-62.

II. ABRAHAM'S READY RESPONSE: IN SPITE OF THE GREAT COST, ABRAHAM UNHESITATINGLY AND UNGRUDGINGLY GAVE GOD HIS BEST; Gen. 22:3-8.
   1. It was to cost Abraham his home life; no child!
   2. It cost him all personal incentive to live.
   Abraham did not hesitate. He made no excuses. He offered no alibis. He rose up early the next morning and entered upon the awful ordeal through which God had called him to pass.

III. ABRAHAM'S NEW DISCOVERY: WHAT ONE PLACES ON GOD'S ALTAR IS NOT LOST AND NEVER CAN BE LOST; Gen. 22:9-12.
   1. Not a hair on the child's head was harmed.
   2. Abraham received back the child he gave to God with the promise that his children would be as numberless as the stars in the heavens.

IV. ABRAHAM'S NEW BEGINNING: FROM THE HOUR HE PLACED HIS BEST ON GOD'S ALTAR, ABRAHAM BEGAN TO RECEIVE GOD'S BEST; Gen. 22:14-19.
   This is also true today. Most of us live and die and never receive God's best things in our lives only because we have never given God our best. Note three things about Abraham.
   1. God brought a new meaning of himself into Abraham's life from this day on; henceforth he was Jehovah-jireh; Gen. 22:14.
   2. God made a new and greater covenant of blessing with Abraham from that day on and took an oath to fulfil it; Gen. 22:15-18.
   3. By His blessings upon Abraham and his descendants, God made it possible for Abraham henceforth to live for the whole wide world; Gen. 22:18.

— E. P. Alldredge

GOING BEYOND THE GARDEN GATE

MATTHEW 26:36-41

INTRODUCTION: Not all Christians are in the same class. Some draw near the Lord in an intimacy about which others never know anything. I want to take the expression, "And He went a little farther," from the thirty-ninth verse of the passage which I have just read and apply it to today. In my judgment, nothing is needed by Christian people any more than to, "go a little farther." Let me go into detail.

I. CHRISTIANS NEED TO GO A LITTLE FARTHER IN SPIRITUALITY.

1. There are many good people in churches who know only a little about real, genuine spirituality of life.

2. People often join a church with no thought of ever backing up or taking part in more than half that the church is trying to do.

3. Christians who are set in their ways and who are accustomed in doing only so much need to go a little farther with the Lord.

II. CHRISTIANS NEED TO GO A LITTLE FARTHER IN REGARD TO THE WILL OF GOD.

1. The most important thing in the life of a Christian is to know and to do the will of God; I John 2:17.

2. Young people will avoid making some dreadful mistakes if they will from the outset of their Christian life seek to know and to follow the will of God; Matt. 6:33.

3. Much of the sickness and most of the unhappiness of life comes about as the direct result of living out of the will of God; Prov. 13:15.

4. Christians need to examine their lives, to find to what extent they seek to know and to follow the will of God.

5. A spiritual church is a church with people who daily seek to know and to follow the will of God.

III. CHRISTIANS NEED TO GO A LITTLE FARTHER IN PRAYER.

1. Our greatest need is not finer buildings; not softer pews, not more style and dignity; but a deeper spirituality in which people come to know what it means to live, walk, and talk with God.

2. The desire of every Christian in his prayer life should be to have a closer walk with the Lord.

— Adapted from Roy Mason

WHAT IS SALVATION?

I PETER 1:10

INTRODUCTION: Somehow the world has failed to see the real meaning of salvation. Salvation is an outstanding Bible doctrine and also the initial Christian experience. Is it not true that the Saints of God need to clearly see what God did for them on the cross when Christ died? Unless believers have a clear knowledge of salvation, they cannot enter into the adequate benefits that it provides. Let us look at the Christian life at its inception and see what we start with the very moment we put our trust in Christ. Now, what is salvation?

I. REDEMPTION FROM DARKNESS; Col. 1:13.
   1. Man has been blinded by Satan, the god of this world; II Cor. 4:3, 4.
   2. Man needs salvation to rescue him from darkness and open his eyes to the new life that is in Christ; Acts 26:18.

II. REDEMPTION FROM SIN; I Peter 1:18.
   1. Redemption in itself means to be born again; John 3:3, 5, 7.
   2. Redemption delivers from the authority of sin and puts one under the Lordship of Jesus Christ; Rom. 6:14.

III. RESURRECTION FROM DEATH; Eph. 2:1.
   1. When a man trusts Christ and believes on Him, he is raised from the dead and made to "sit together in heavenly places in Christ Jesus"; Eph. 2:5, 6.
   2. Sin has killed us spiritually; faith in Christ raises us out of the grave of spiritual death and gives us Divine life.

IV. RETURN FROM EXILE; Eph. 2:13.
   1. One thing that sin did when it invaded the Garden of Eden was to separate man from God; Isa. 59:2.
   2. Across the distance of separation from God, man can call on God; Acts 2:21.
   3. Salvation through the blood of Christ, brings man home from exile to walk with God; Eph. 2:13.

V. RELEASES FROM CAPTIVITY; Rom. 6:6.
   1. Man without Christ is bound by the chain of sin; Mark 5:1-5.
   2. Salvation makes it possible for man to be free to live for the Saviour, free to serve the Saviour, and free to enjoy the Saviour; John 8:32; Mark 5:15.

— Adapted from Andrew Telford in *The Gospel Herald*

EVERY MAN'S WORK SHALL BE TRIED

I CORINTHIANS 3:13; REVELATION 20:13

INTRODUCTION: These Scriptures are addressed to two different classes of people. The first is to the saved and the other to the unsaved. They will not be judged at the same time. The Scripture teaches that the Thousand Year Reign of Christ will separate their judgments.

I. THE WORKS OF GOD'S CHILDREN WILL BE TRIED OR PUT TO A TEST.
   1. Christians will be judged at the Judgment Seat of Christ; II Cor. 5:10.
   2. This will be a judgment of the believer's works, not his soul.
      a. A test of obedience to the faith once delivered to the Saints; Judg. 3.
      b. A test of fidelity to Christ as a practical Christian.
   3. This judgment of believers will determine their rewards. Reward is recompense for work done; Rev. 22:12. Some will have no reward.
   4. There are many rewards mentioned in the Bible.
      a. Prize of the high calling; Phil. 3:14.
      b. Reward of inheritance; Col. 3:24.
      c. Heirs of the Kingdom; James 2:5.
      d. Crown of life; James 1:12; Rev. 2:10.
      e. Crown of righteousness; II Tim. 4:8.
      f. Crown of glory; I Peter 5:4.
      g. Incorruptible crown; I Cor. 9:25.

II. THERE IS ALSO A JUDGMENT FOR THE UNBELIEVER AND HIS WORKS.
   1. This is called the Great White Throne Judgment; Rev. 20:11.
      a. It is a throne of eternal justice.
      b. It is no human court; Rev. 20:12.
      c. Here records are examined; Rev. 20:12; Dan. 7:10.
   2. At this judgment the sinner receives the final sentence for the condemnation already passed upon him. Note why a sinner is condemned; John 3:18.
   3. The sinner is sentenced to the lake of fire; Rev. 20:15.

III. WHAT IF YOUR WORKS WERE TRIED TODAY?
   Let us use this fourfold test.
      a. Will your belief satisfy the highest demands of your conscience?
      b. Will your belief release you from sin in this life?
      c. Will your belief meet the needs of your soul at death?
      d. Will your belief meet the issue when you stand in judgment?

— L. Chester Guinn

WHAT THE BIBLE TEACHES ABOUT ETERNAL LIFE
JOHN 3:16

INTRODUCTION: It is of far greater importance to know what the Scriptures teach concerning eternal life, than to know how long we can live, or how much money we can make, or how much of this world we can see.

I. IT IS DESIRED.

"And, behold, one came and said unto him, Good Master, what good thing shall I do, that I may have eternal life?" Matt. 19:16.

II. IT IS PROMISED.

"And this is the promise that he hath promised us, even eternal life." I John 2:25.
"In hope of eternal life, which God, that cannot lie, promised before the world began." Titus 1:2.

III. IT IS IN GOD'S SON.

"And we know that the Son of God is come, and hath given us an understanding, that we may know him that is true, and we are in him that is true, even in his Son Jesus Christ. This is the true God, and eternal life." I John 5:20; 1:1-3.

IV. IT IS A GIFT.

"For the wages of sin is death; but the gift of God is eternal life through Jesus Christ our Lord." Rom. 6:23; cf. John 10:28; 17:2; I John 5:11.

V. IT IS RECEIVED BY FAITH.

"But as many as received him, to them gave he power to become the sons of God, even to them that believe on his name." John 1:12; 3:16; Acts 13:48.

VI. IT IS A PRESENT POSSESSION.

"He that hath the Son hath life; and he that hath not the Son of God hath not life." I John 5:12, 13; John 6:54.

VII. IT IS TO BE LAID HOLD UPON.

"Fight the good fight of faith, lay hold on eternal life, whereunto thou art also called, and hast professed a good profession before many witnesses." I Tim. 6:12, 19.

— William H. Schweinfurth

THE THRONE OF GOD

PSALM 45:6

INTRODUCTION: Earthly thrones are established and likewise pass away, but the throne of God is established forever and ever. Some have probably asked, "What does the throne of God signify?" Let me tell you from God's Word what the throne of God signifies.

I. THE THRONE OF GOD SIGNIFIES SOVEREIGNTY.

1. God is sovereign in that He can say that Heaven is His throne and the earth His footstool; Isa. 66:1.
2. Nebuchadnezzar learned about God's sovereignty as a result of God's dealing with him; Dan. 4:30-37.

II. THE THRONE OF GOD SIGNIFIES HOLINESS.

1. God is a holy God; Ps. 47:8.
2. God's holiness caused the seraphims to cover their faces while in His presence; Isa. 6:2, 3.
3. Because of His holiness God could not bear to look at sin when it was laid on His Son, the Lord Jesus Christ; Hab. 1:13; Matt. 27:45.

III. THE THRONE OF GOD SIGNIFIES WRATH.

1. God, besides being a God of love is also a God of wrath; John 3:16; Rom. 1:18.
2. Men who have rejected Christ will cry for the mountains (and rocks) to fall on them and hide them from God's wrath; Rev. 6:16, 17.

IV. THE THRONE OF GOD SIGNIFIES JUDGMENT.

1. God has a reservation at the Great White Throne Judgment for Christ rejectors; Rev. 20:11, 12a.
2. Every event in an unsaved person's life, including the secrets of their life, will be opened before God at the Great White Throne Judgment; Rev. 20: 12b-15.

V. THE THRONE OF GOD SIGNIFIES GRACE.

1. God's children are invited to come boldly to the throne of grace to find help for their daily needs; Heb. 4:16.
2. Grace from God's throne makes it possible for a sinner to be saved; Eph. 2:8, 9.

— Adapted from John R. Gilpin

OUT OF CHRIST BY NATURE AND INTO CHRIST BY GRACE
EPHESIANS 2:1-13

I. WITHOUT CHRIST IS THE CONDITION OF ALL MEN BY NATURE; Eph. 2:1-3.

1. Out of Christ means that an individual has:

   a. No Christ; Rom. 8:9.

   b. No life. All is death outside of Him; I John 5:12; John 3:36.

   c. No peace, but blackness of despair forever; Rom. 3:17.

   d. No excuse. God's Word is too plain; Rom. 1:20.

   e. No escape. Neglect will send the poor soul into Hell; II Peter 3:9.

II. THE WAY INTO CHRIST; Eph. 1:13.

1. By the way of repentance; Acts 20:21.

   a. Repentance was the message of John the Baptist; Matt. 3:2.

   b. Repentance was the message of Christ; Mark 1:15; Luke 13:3-5.

   c. Repentance was prescribed by Paul; Acts 17:30, 31.

2. There are three elements in true repentance.

   a. Conviction. To realize you are a sinner.

   b. Contrition. Sorrow for sin.

   c. Conversion. Change from sin.

3. The three elements in true conversion are shown in the conversion of the Philippian Jailer; Acts 16:29-33.

   a. Conviction. "...came trembling,..." Realizing he was a sinner.

   b. Contrition. "...fell down before Paul and Silas,...and said, Sirs, what must I do to be saved?"

   c. Conversion. "...he took them the same hour of the night, and washed their stripes; and was baptized, he and all his, straightway." Changed from sin.

4. The way into Christ is by the way of faith; Acts 20:21.

   a. Faith is toward Jesus Christ. He satisfies the law which we had broken.

   b. There are two elements in true faith.

      (1) Belief; John 3:16; Heb. 11:6.

      (2) Trust; II Tim. 1:12.

                                        — Adapted from L. Chester Guinn

25

THE WAY OF SALVATION

TITUS 3:5

I. **SALVATION IS NOT EFFECTED BY HUMAN AGENCY.**
   1. Where there is no salvation, there are no works of righteousness; Gen. 6:5; Gal. 5:19-21.
   2. Works of righteousness, even where they exist, possess no saving effect.
   3. The Bible disclaims the merit of human agency in salvation; Isa. 64:6; Dan. 9:7; Rom. 3:20-28; 11:5, 6; Gal. 2:21; Eph. 2:8, 9.

II. **SALVATION ORIGINATES IN THE DIVINE COMPASSION.** "According to His mercy He saved us."
   1. Our salvation accords with the tender sympathies attributed to that mercy; Pss. 25:6; 51:1; Isa. 63:15; Luke 1:78; James 5:11.
   2. It accords with the readiness ascribed to that mercy; Neh. 9:17; Isa. 30:18; Mic. 7:18.
   3. It accords with the description given of the greatness, fulness, and extent of that mercy; Num. 14:19; Ps. 5:7; Neh. 9:19; Pss. 119:64; 145:9.
   4. It accords with the perpetuity of that mercy; Ps. 118:1.

III. **SALVATION IS ATTENDED BY AN IMPORTANT CHANGE.**
   1. Delivered from the love of sinful pleasures and carnal delights, by having the "love of God shed abroad in our hearts"; Rom. 5:5.
   2. From the guilt of sinful practices, by having a knowledge of salvation by the remission of sins.
   3. From the prevalence of sinful habits, by the principles of holiness, and the power of the Divine Spirit.
   4. From the commission of sinful acts, by the total regeneration of our natures; I John 5:18.

IV. **SALVATION IS ACCOMPLISHED BY A DIVINE INFLUENCE.** "By the renewing of the Holy Ghost."
   1. The light and information which we receive on Divine subjects are communicated by the Holy Ghost; John 14:26; I Cor. 2:11, 12; I John 2:20.
   2. The conviction we have of our personal danger is derived from the same source; John 16:8.
   3. The change which is produced in the minds of Christian believers is attributed to the Holy Ghost; John 3:5-8; I Cor. 6:11; II Cor. 3:18.
   4. The assurance of salvation is by the witness of the Holy Ghost — the Comforter; John 14:16; Rom. 8:16.

— Sketches of Sermons in *The Biblical Illustrator*

THE PREACHING OF THE CROSS

I CORINTHIANS 1:18

INTRODUCTION: Our text is in verse 18, "For the preaching of the cross is to them that perish foolishness; but unto us which are saved, it is the power of God." There are four things about the cross that I want us to consider.

I. THE PREACHING OF THE CROSS SWEEPS AWAY MAN'S PRETENSES.
   1. It sweeps aside all of man's pretenses of being good outside of Jesus; Rom. 3:23; Isa. 53:6.
   2. It sweeps aside man's pretenses of being saved by works; Eph. 2:8, 9.

II. THE PREACHING OF THE CROSS REVEALS THE LOVE AND GRACE OF GOD.
   1. The greatest revelation, the greatest demonstration, the greatest exhibition of the love and grace of God is the crucifixion of Jesus.
      a. At the cross man is seen at his worst and God's grace is seen at its best.
      b. At the cross man's crime is seen and God's compassion is seen.
      c. At the cross man's ruin is seen and God's redemption is seen.
   2. The cross reveals that Jesus did not die for good people but that He died for sinners; Rom. 5:8.

III. THE PREACHING OF THE CROSS SHOWS THE WAY OF SALVATION.
   1. It shows the way of forgiveness; Col. 2:13.
   2. It shows the way to God; Acts 4:12.
   3. It shows the way to Heaven; John 14:5.
   4. It shows the way to peace; Rom. 5:1.
   5. It shows the way out of Hell; Rom. 5:8-10.

IV. THE PREACHING OF THE CROSS DIVIDES THE WORLD INTO TWO GROUPS.
   1. The saved side.
      a. On one side was the thief who said, "Lord, remember me when thou comest into thy kingdom"; Luke 23:42.
      b. The man on this side of the cross was saved and went to Heaven.
   2. The condemned side.
      a. On the other side was the thief who cried, "If thou be Christ, save thyself and us"; Luke 23:39.
      b. The man on this side of the cross was lost and went to Hell.

— Adapted from Tom Malone

THE PENITENT THIEF

LUKE 23:27-45

INTRODUCTION: This portion of Scripture should awaken every sinner to the need of salvation. Jesus saved this poor, undeserving thief in His dying hour. "For this cause came I into the world"; John 18:37.

I. THE SETTING.
1. Christ hanging on the cross; Vs. 33.
2. A malefactor on each side; Vs. 33; Isa. 53:12; Ps. 22:16.
3. The mocking crowd; deriding and casting lots; Vs. 34-36.
   Matthew tells us (27:44), that "the thieves also which were crucified with him, cast the same in his teeth." The first thing we see of the thief, then, was that he was a reviler of Christ.

II. THE SUDDEN CHANGE.
1. He heard Jesus' prayer; Vs. 34. He heard Him pray for sinners and knew that he was included. Prayer changes things.
2. He defended the Saviour; Vs. 41.
3. He rebuked his friend; Vs. 40.

III. THE SINNER'S CONFESSION.
1. He confessed his unworthiness; Vs. 41a. "We indeed justly."
2. He confessed the Saviour's worthiness; Vs. 41b. "Nothing amiss."
3. He confessed his faith in Christ; Vs. 42; Rom. 10:17.
   This is one of the greatest acts of faith in the Bible. He had little worldly evidence to prove that Jesus was King, yet he believed the superscription that said he was. The only throne he could see, was a cross. The only crown he could see, was a crown of thorns. The only sceptre visible to him, was a reed, placed in Jesus' hand by a mocker. The only subjects he saw, were those to whom Jesus had become subject.

IV. THE SAVIOUR'S PROMISE.
1. He promised him salvation; Vs. 43.
2. He promised it immediately; Vs. 43.
3. He promised him a home with Him; Vs. 43; John 14:3.

— Lewis Button

28

THE BACKSLIDER

PROVERBS 14:14; JEREMIAH 2:19

I. WHAT IS A BACKSLIDER?
  1. A backslider is a saved person who falls into sin; Judg. 16:20.
  2. There are some individuals in the Bible who 'are not considered as backsliders because they were not born again when they indulged in sin.
      a. Adam, when he fell into sin in the Garden of Eden, was not a backslider.
      b. Fallen angels are not backsliders.
      c. Judas Iscariot was not a backslider; John 6:64, 70, 71.

II. WHY PEOPLE BACKSLIDE?
The reason that people backslide is because of the old carnal nature. This nature is not eradicated when the new birth is received; Rom. 7:14-25.
  1. It is easier to do wrong than it is to do right.
  2. It is easier to loaf than it is to work.
  3. It is easier to get angry than it is to be eventempered, forgiving and sweet.

III. THE SORROWS OF BACKSLIDING.
  1. The backslider is sure of the chastising of God; Heb. 12:5, 6.
      a. For David's sin, God smote his child, and it died.
      b. When the Saints at Corinth got drunk at the Lord's Table, God brought judgment; I Cor. 11:30.
  2. The backslider reaps the natural wages of sin; Gal. 6:7, 8.
  3. The backslider will have the remorse of conscience over his sins; Ps. 51.
  4. The backslider must appear before the Judgment Seat of Christ; II Cor. 5:10; I Cor. 3:12-15.

IV. THE BACKSLIDER; SAVED OR LOST.
  1. God promises to all who believe in Christ "everlasting life." John 3:36; 5:24; 6:47.
  2. The backslider is a disobedient Child of God.
  3. God never forsakes one of His children, even though we sin grievously and though He may punish us severely; Ps. 89:30-34.

V. HOW TO GET BACK INTO FULL FELLOWSHIP WITH GOD.
  1. Simply turn to God, confessing your sin; I John 1:9.
  2. To stay in fellowship, when a sin appears, confess it quickly to God, asking Him to forgive it; I John 1:7.

— Adapted from John R. Rice

29

JESUS ON TRIAL
MATTHEW 16:13-20

INTRODUCTION: In court, witnesses are brought forth to testify. (Explain our court procedure.) Is Jesus what or who He claimed to be? That is, is He the Son of God?

I. THE TESTIMONY OF CHRIST'S FRIENDS.
1. Prophecy declares it to be so; Isa. 7:14; 9:6.
2. The Twelve acknowledged Him; Matt. 16:16.

II. THE TESTIMONY OF DEITY.
1. God spoke from Heaven twice; Matt. 3:17; 17:5.
2. Jesus' testimony before the high priest; Mark 14:60-62.

III. THE TESTIMONY OF THE ENEMY.
1. Devils testified that He was the Son of God; Matt. 8:29; Luke 4:34.
2. At the trial Pilate said, "He is innocent." Luke 23:14.
3. The centurion's testimony who was in charge of the crucifixion; Luke 23:47.
4. The Sandhedrin knew Him to be the Son of God, for they bribed the guard to falsify His resurrection; Matt. 28:11-14.
5. On Pentecost three thousand enemies became members of the first church at Jerusalem; Acts 2.
6. Saul of Tarsus, the arch-enemy of the church, became the greatest apostle; Acts 9.

IV. JESUS WAS NOT AN IMPOSTER.
1. The angels brought the good news to the shepherds; Luke 2:10-14.
2. Astronomy declared His birth to the wise men; Matt. 2:1, 2.
3. Martyrs have died for His cause. (Cf. History).
4. The saved are a living evidence.

V. JESUS IS ON TRIAL TODAY AS NEVER BEFORE.
1. The organized forces of Hell are fighting Him; Ps. 2:1-3.
2. As false witnesses were brought against Jesus, today false witnesses are raging against the cardinal principles of the New Testament.
   a. Attacking the Bible itself.
   b. Attacking Christ's Deity and Virgin Birth.

VI. LOST SOUL, JESUS IS ON TRIAL IN YOUR HEART.
1. Will you not desert the ranks of the enemy and come confessing Jesus as your Saviour? Rom. 10:10.
2. Friend, if you are a Christian and out of service, will you not let Jesus have His rightful place in your life, that the joy of your salvation may be restored.

— Adapted from C. L. Jones

THE GREAT NECESSITY
JOHN 3:3, 5

I. THE NATURE OF THE NEW BIRTH.
1. Negatively:
   a. Not a second natural birth, as Nicodemus supposed.
   b. Not baptism with water, much less sprinkling.
   c. Not external reformation.
   d. Not confirmation.
   e. Not joining one of the numerous sects; this is only a hiding place for many who do not want to follow Jesus.
2. Positively:
   a. It is a re-creation; John 1:13; 3:3, 5.
   b. It is a resurrection; Eph. 2:1; I John 3:14.
   c. It is a translation; Col. 1:13.
   d. It is a transformation; Rom. 12:2.
   e. It is an impartation — new heart, Ezek. 36:26 — new nature, II Peter 1:4.

II. THE NECESSITY OF THE NEW BIRTH.
1. To communion with God; light no fellowship with darkness; sin with holiness; Christ with Satan; II Cor. 6:14-18.
2. To an interest in the promises; estate is for children; Rom. 8:17.
3. To holiness; no one can be holy without a holy nature; II Peter 1:4.
4. To acceptable obedience; our prayers, praise, works — abomination; Prov. 21:27.
5. To true membership with His church on earth; His family; Eph. 3:15.
6. To an entrance into Heaven; Heaven a holy place, the home of God's children.

III. THE MEANS OF REGENERATION.
1. The efficient means is the Spirit of God; it is the peculiar prerogative of God, by His Holy Spirit. "you hath he quickened"; Eph. 2:1.
2. The instrumental means is the Word of God; I Peter 1:23; James 1:18.

IV. THE EVIDENCE.
1. Faith; I John 5:1.
2. Victory over the world; I John 5:4.
3. Righteousness of life; I John 5:18; 3:9.
4. Love to God and the brethren; I John 4:7, 20; 5:1, 2.

CONCLUSION: This subject should lead to serious self-examination. To diligent searching after God.

— Frederick Rader

31

NAAMAN, THE LEPER
II KINGS 5
GOLDEN TEXT: I CORINTHIANS 1:18

I. HIS DESCRIPTION; Vs. 1.
1. Position; "captain." The commander-in-chief.
2. Power; "great man." Authority, popularity and great influence.
3. Character; "honorable." Cultured, refined, gracious, a gentleman.
4. Victory; "deliverance." He had rid Syria of foreign dominance.
5. Bravery; "valour." Fearless in the fight.
6. The fearful "but a leper." Note the result of leprosy.
   a. Leprosy separated him.
   b. Leprosy rendered him unclean.
   c. Leprosy rendered him incurable by human means.
   d. Leprosy would eventually bring him to death.

II. HIS OPPORTUNITY; Vss. 2, 3.
1. The little maid's capture. Taken from home, friends, care, etc.
2. Her purchaser; Vs. 2. Naaman's wife.
3. Her faith; Vs. 3. In the midst of idolatry she shone for the living God.

III. HIS MISTAKES; Vss. 4-11.
1. He went to the wrong person; Vss. 3-7.
2. He went with the wrong means; Vs. 5. Gold, silver, and raiment; Eph. 2:8, 9.
3. He went with the wrong idea; Vs. 11.

IV. HIS ATTITUDE; Vss. 10-13.
1. The message, through the servant; Vs. 10; Acts 16:30, 31.
2. Naaman lost his temper; Vs. 11. God's way is always down! Luke 18:14; I Cor. 1:27-29.
3. The reason; Vs. 13. Nothing unreasonable in God's way; Isa. 1:18.

V. HIS CURE; Vs. 14.
1. He lost his pride. Good riddance to bad rubbish! Note: He went down.
2. He lost his leprosy. Picture the scene and his feelings as he realized the glorious truth of his cleansing.

VI. HIS TESTIMONY; Vss. 15-19.
1. "I know." I John 5:13; John 5:24; Rom. 1:16; II Tim. 1:12.
2. Do you know or hope?
   — From *Through the Scriptures* by Alfred P. Gibbs by kind permission of Faithful Words Publishing Co., 2116 S. Jefferson St., St. Louis 4, Missouri

THE DOCTRINE OF THE NEW BIRTH

JOHN 3:5

I. THE MEANING OF THE NEW BIRTH.
  1. What it is not.
     a. It is not baptism; I Cor. 4:15; I Cor. 1:14, 17.
     b. It is not reformation; John 3:3-6.
  2. What it is.
     a. A spiritual generation; II Peter 1:4; I Peter 1:23.
     b. A spiritual quickening or resurrection; Eph. 2:1, 5, 6.
        (1) Through sin, man's spirit came into a condition of spiritual death.
        (2) In regeneration man is quickened out of his spiritual separation and disunion into a spiritual life of union and communion with God.
        (3) Resurrection is the restoration to life of that which life has become extinct.
     c. A spiritual translation; Col. 1:13.
        (1) Regeneration is a transfer from one kingdom to another.
        (2) Regeneration is the transfer from the kingdom of darkness, in which sin and Satan rule, into the Kingdom of God's Dear Son.
     d. A spiritual creation; Eph. 2:10.

II. THE NECESSITY OF THE NEW BIRTH.
  1. Because of the inability of that which belongs to one kingdom or order to enter another by itself unaided; John 3:3-7.
  2. Because of man's condition of spiritual death; Eph. 2:1.

III. THE OLD NATURE IS NOT ERADICATED BY THE NEW BIRTH.
  1. Every Christian has two natures, the old nature and the new nature.
  2. The theory that one can have a second experience in which the old Adamic nature is completely removed is both contrary to Scripture and human observation.
     a. Paul said that he had a struggle with the flesh all the time; I Cor. 9:27.
     b. The warfare between the old nature and the new nature never ends this side of death.
  3. The reason why so many Church members have no spiritual appetite, endure only for a short time and then drop out, and are worldly in impulse and desire is the lack of the New Birth.

— Adapted from Fred T. Halliman

33

JESUS, THE MIGHTY TO SAVE

HEBREWS 7:25

INTRODUCTION:

1. It is possible to view this great text from the standpoint of the sinner who is "saved unto the uttermost." This is certainly a great theme.
2. This text and the context deals with Jesus and His great power to save, and save unto the uttermost, all who come to God by Him. Let us follow the text, therefore, and think together about Jesus the mighty to save:

I. JESUS IS MIGHTY TO SAVE BECAUSE HE CAME FOR THAT SPECIAL PURPOSE.

1. The angel announcing His birth said He would save the people from their sins; Luke 1:31-35; 2:10-12.
2. Over and over again Jesus told His disciples that He had come to save; John 3:14-17; 6:30; 6:40; 10:9, 10; Luke 19:10.

II. JESUS IS MIGHTY TO SAVE BECAUSE HE MADE THE WORLD AND THE SOULS OF MEN; John 1:3.

1. Jesus is the Great Physician who is able to heal with a word.
2. Jesus is the Great Teacher who can give light and life to all; John 1:8-13.
3. Jesus is the great Maker and Ruler of the universe and knows how to remake individuals in his own image.

III. JESUS IS MIGHTY TO SAVE BECAUSE HE "TASTED DEATH FOR EVERY MAN," AND MADE A COMPLETE ATONEMENT FOR ALL SIN.

1. He is the Lamb of God that takes away the sin of the world; John 1:29, 35.
2. He suffered for all men that all who would believe might be saved; Heb. 2:9; John 3:14-17; I John 2:2.
3. He became a great High Priest of God who offered Himself for our sins and now intercedes for us; Heb. 7:23-27.

IV. JESUS IS MIGHTY TO SAVE BECAUSE HE OVERCAME ALL THE FOES OF THE HUMAN SOUL TO BECOME THE COMPLETE AND PERFECT SAVIOUR.

1. He overcame Satan in the wilderness temptation; Luke 4:1-15.
2. He met the world and overcame it; John 16:33.
3. He overcame opposing forces in the Garden of Gethsemane; Luke 22:39-46.
4. He overcame sin by living a pure life and by His death on the cross; Heb. 9:26-28; I Peter 2:22-24.
5. He overcame death by His resurrection; I Cor. 15:20-28.

— Adapted from E. P. Alldredge

THOSE WHO SEEK THE LORD

ISAIAH 55:6

I. THEY SHALL FIND GOD AND LIVE; Jer. 29:13; Amos 5:5.

"And ye shall seek me, and find me, when ye shall search for me with all your heart." Cf. Deut. 4:29.

"For thus saith the Lord unto the house of Israel, Seek ye me, and ye shall live." Cf. II Chron. 15:2.

II. THEY SHALL REJOICE; Ps. 105:3.

"Glory ye in his holy name: let the heart of them rejoice that seek the Lord." Cf. Pss. 40:16; 70:4.

III. THEY SHALL UNDERSTAND; Prov. 28:5.

"Evil men understand not judgment: but they that seek the Lord understand all things."

IV. THEY SHALL NOT WANT; Ps. 34:10.

"The young lions do lack, and suffer hunger: but they that seek the Lord shall not want any good thing."

V. THEY SHALL NOT BE CONFOUNDED; Ps. 69:6.

"Let not them that wait on thee, O Lord God of hosts, be ashamed for my sake: let not those that seek thee be confounded for my sake, O God of Israel."

VI. THEY SHALL NOT BE FORSAKEN; Ps. 9:10.

"And they that know thy name will put their trust in thee: for thou, Lord, hast not forsaken them that seek thee."

VII. THEY SHALL BE BLESSED; Ezra 8:22.

"The hand of our God is upon all them for good that seek him; but his power and his wrath is against all them that forsake him."

VIII. THEY SHALL BE GREATLY REWARDED; Heb. 11:6.

"But without faith it is impossible to please him: for he that cometh to God must believe that he is, and that he is a rewarder of them that diligently seek him."

— William H. Schweinfurth

DYING WITH THE PHILISTINES

JUDGES 16:30

INTRODUCTION: Today, professing Christians are devoting much of their time and energies to the work of Satan rather than to the service of our Saviour. It is shocking to think of the professing Christians who are dying daily around the world with the Philistines of Satan! Now, let us consider in detail the case of Samson as it is presented to us in the Book of Judges.

I. THE WORTH OF SAMSON.

1. Samson had great potential and ability that could have been used for the Lord in a glorious way.
   a. He was born in answer to prayer; Judg. 13:8, 9.
   b. He was a Nazarite as was our Lord Jesus Christ; Judg. 13:7.

2. The only true measure of any Christian's value to the cause of Christ is what he could do with the power of God's Holy Spirit resting upon him.

II. THE WEAKNESS OF SAMSON.

1. Samson's strength could have been his greatest asset; but it proved to be, in the final analysis, his greatest weakness.

2. In most cases, people who know the Saviour and who are defeated, discouraged and dejected are those who have sought to solve their problems through the flesh rather than through the power of the Holy Spirit; John 6:63.

3. God is not pleased when we depend upon our own strength and ability and fail to walk with Him by faith; Heb. 11:6.

4. Many church members today, have lost their power with the Lord and their testimony because of worldliness and their courtship of the ungodly.

III. THE WASTE OF SAMSON.

1. Samson was busy throwing his life away and squandering the talents that God had intrusted to him at a time when Israel sorely needed a godly man to call the nation to repentance.

2. In order for Christians to avoid a waste of life, time and talents, they need to give heed to God's admonition not to be unequally yoked together with unbelievers; II Cor. 6:14-17.

— Adapted from Robert Gray

FROM BLINDNESS TO BELIEF
LUKE 18:35-43

I. CONDITION.

1. Blind; Vs. 35. "A certain blind man"; II Cor. 4:3, 4; John 3:3. The unsaved are spiritually blind. They have:
   a. Blind leaders; Matt. 15:14. They cannot be led aright.
   b. Blind minds; II Cor. 3:14. They cannot think aright.
   c. Blindness of heart; Eph.4:18. They cannot love God aright.
   d. Blind eyes; I John 2:11. They cannot see the truth.

2. Begging; Vs. 35; "Sat by the wayside begging."
   a. The reasons for such soul poverty.
      (1) Lust; Prov. 21:17; I Tim. 5:6; II Tim. 3:4; Heb. 11:25; Ps. 16:11.
      (2) Laziness; Prov. 23:21; I Thess. 5:6; Eph. 5:14.
      (3) Leaders; Prov. 28:19; Acts 20:29-32.
   b. The realization of such soul poverty.
      (1) Difficult, it is possible to be poor and not know it; Rev. 3:17.
      (2) Deduced, by the Scripture; Ps. 119:130; by the Spirit of God; John 3:5-8.

II. CONVICTION.

1. He heard; Vs. 36. "And hearing the multitude."; Rom. 10:17; John 5:24; Isa. 53:3.

2. He hurried immediately; Vs. 37, 40. II Cor. 6:2; Prov. 27:1; James 2:20; Mark 3:13; Rom. 8:29, 30; Matt. 11:28; John 6:37.

III. CONVERSION.

1. The request; Vs. 40, 41. "Lord." Phil. 2:10; John 10:9 Rom. 10:9, 13.

2. The response; Vs. 42.
   a. The means, "Jesus said." John 6:47.
   b. The manner, "receive"; John 1:12; I Cor. 4:47; Rom. 6:23.
   c. The might, "saved" Personal faith — progressive faith; Eph. 2:8.
   d. The moment, present salvation — "saved"; I John 3:14; 5:13; John 3:36; Titus 3:5, 6.

3. The result; Vs. 43.
   a. Cured — "received his sight"; Isa. 45:22; John 1:29; Heb. 2:9; 12:2.
   b. Converted — "followed Him"; Heb. 10:25, 26; Acts 9:26; Rev. 14:4; John 8:12.
   c. Confessing — "glorifying God"; Ps. 50:23; Matt. 10:32, 33; Gal. 3:27; Rom. 6:3, 4.

— Adapted from Frank Beck

JESUS, THE LIGHT OF THE WORLD
JOHN 8:12

I. JESUS IS THE LIGHT OF THE INTELLECTUAL WORLD.
   1. I would rather sit at the feet of a woman who lives in a cabin and who can scarcely write her name, but who knows Jesus, than to sit at the feet of the greatest scholar the world ever saw, if that scholar is not a Christian; I Cor. 1:21.
   2. Jesus not only comes into your heart when you are saved, but He also stimulates your faculties. He helps you see.

II. JESUS IS THE LIGHT OF THE SOCIAL WORLD.
   1. Jesus made womanhood all that is in this country.
   2. Jesus made childhood all that it is in the world. He touched babyhood into beauty; Mark 10:14.

III. JESUS IS THE LIGHT OF THE RELIGIOUS WORLD.
   1. A Christian is a person who, knowing that he cannot save himself, relies upon Jesus Christ and His atoning blood for salvation.
   2. The Christian religion is a religion of song. It is Jesus who puts a song into the heart; I Cor. 15:55.

IV. JESUS IS THE LIGHT OF THIS DARK WORLD.
   1. There was light wherever Jesus was.
   2. At Calvary, the light flashed into the heart of the dying thief. It got rid of all darkness of his soul and got it ready to go Home to God.

V. JESUS IS THE LIGHT OF THE ETERNAL HEAVEN.
   1. Think of a city where shadows never come. There evening twilight nor morning twilight ever comes; it is always noonday splendor.
   2. Think of living in an eternal city where there were no graveyards, where nobody died, where no babies ever cried in pain, where nobody wore mourning clothes.

VI. JESUS MAY BECOME THE LIGHT OF THE INDIVIDUAL WORLD.
   1. Trust Jesus Christ; yield your life to Him and He will turn all your tears into pearls, string them for you, put them in a crown of joy and put the crown on your head.
   2. Trust Jesus Christ and He will chase away the midnight darkness. He can drive the darkness out of the valley of the shadow of death; Ps. 23:4.

— Bob Jones, Sr.

GOD'S CALL TO SERVICE

ISAIAH 6

INTRODUCTION: This chapter records the experience Isaiah had when he was initiated into the prophetic office. It was a thrilling and awe-inspiring experience. After Isaiah was divinely cleansed from his sin, Jehovah inquired whom He would send, and Isaiah voluntarily heeded the call and yielded himself to the service of the Lord. We have in this passage the call of Jehovah and Isaiah's response to that call.

I. WE OBSERVE JEHOVAH'S CALL. Vs. 8, "Whom shall I send, and who will go for us?"

1. It will be observed that it is the Triune God who is looking for messengers to carry and proclaim His message. "Us."
   a. That the Godhead exists as a Trinity is not a matter of human speculation but of Divine revelation; Rom. 1:19, 20.
   b. That fact that the being of God consists in the threefold relationship of Father, Son and Holy Spirit can, however, not be known through conscience, neither through the created universe, but only through Scripture revelation.

2. It will be noted that in the Old Testament revelation concerning the Godhead the emphasis always is upon the unity of God; Deut. 6:4; Isa. 44:6; Exod. 20:3.

3. It will likewise be observed that in the New Testament revelation concerning the Godhead, the emphasis is upon the Trinity; Luke 1:35; Eph. 2:18; II Cor. 13:14.

4. The God of Scripture is beyond question a triune being and He is looking for human messengers to carry His message; Luke 24:46-48; Acts 1:8; II Cor. 5:18-21.

II. WE NOTE ISAIAH'S RESPONSE TO JEHOVAH'S CALL. Vs. 8 "Here am I; send me."

1. We note that self-surrender to the Lord is essential in order to do service for the Lord; Acts 8:6; Rom. 6:13; 12:1, 2.

2. We observe that self-surrender should be associated with resolution to be true to the call and commission of the Lord.
   a. The message He is called upon to proclaim is not generally accepted, and never accepted by all, and especially not in these days, the days of foretold apostasy; I Tim. 4:1-3; II Tim. 4:3, 4.
   b. The self-surrender of the servant of the Lord Jesus Christ must have in it a deep measure of Spirit-created faithfulness to the Lord and His blessed Word; Acts 20:24; 27:23; II Tim. 4:2-5.
   — W. S. Hottel in *The Bible Expositor and Illuminator*

WHY PENTECOST?

ACTS 1:8

INTRODUCTION: Did the world need Pentecost? The political world was wicked; Nero's sword was bathed in blood. The moral and social life was corrupt. The religious world was formal; pharisaical emptiness and pagan idolatry had nothing to offer but wickedness and broken hearts. Did the disciples need Pentecost? Every follower of Christ needed it; they were moral and spiritual cowards. They shut themselves in the upper room. Surely they felt their need of it. They had a task to do and they were too weak to do it. The Master told them that they should not depart from Jerusalem, but wait for the promise of the Father. They needed Divine energy. Notice three things in the text:

I. THE PROMISE. "But ye shall receive power, after that the Holy Ghost is come upon you."
  1. The promise of power is given and within it is the thought of authority or dynamic.
  2. In obedience to the Master's command the early believers waited patiently, prayerfully and purposefully; Luke 24:29.
  3. The obedience of the early believers was not in vain; Acts 2:1-4; 4:8-10.
  4. The Holy Spirit indwells every believer today, to produce mighty works; John 14:17; Acts 8:29; 10:19, 20.

II. THE PURPOSE. "Ye shall be witnesses unto me."
  1. At Pentecost power was received to witness by life and by lips; II Cor. 3:2; Acts 8:4.
  2. At Pentecost power was received to testify courageously; Acts 4:21.
  3. At Pentecost power was received to live victoriously; Rom. 6:14.
  4. At Pentecost power was received to live fervently; Rom. 5:5.
  5. At Pentecost power was received to pray effectively; Acts 12:5-19.
  6. At Pentecost power was received to cause individuals to give in a generous way; I Cor. 16:2.

III. THE PLACE. "Ye shall be witnesses unto Me both in Jerusalem, and in Judaea, and in Samaria, and unto the uttermost part of the earth."
  1. Jesus said, "The field is the world; . . ." Matt. 13:38.
  2. Jesus said, ". . . Go ye into all the world, . . ." Mark 16:15.
  3. The Apostle John said, ". . . the whole world lieth in wickedness." I John 5:19.
  4. This revolting world ruined by sin needs our witness. Only Christ can deliver it. Oh, for a new experience of the power of Pentecost.

— Adapted from Andrew Telford in *The Gospel Herald*

SIN AND ITS PUNISHMENT
GOD'S JUSTICE, DEGREES IN HELL
ROMANS 3:23; HEBREWS 2:2; ISAIAH 45:21; MATTHEW 11:24

INTRODUCTION: God is just. Yet, lurking in the minds of multitudes is a vague suspicion or dread that God will be unjust in sending some to Hell, and that He will be unjust in the way He will punish unsaved individuals. Whatever God does in regard to the lost, one thing is certain, He will do no injustice.

I. SIN MUST BE PUNISHED.
1. Just punishment means degrees of punishment; Heb. 2:2.
   a. Sin ought to be punished because it is right to punish it; Rom. 1:18.
   b. How clearly the Lord taught this truth; Matt. 11:20-24.
   c. Paul taught this same truth; Gal. 6:7.
2. Punishment is according to light and opportunity; Luke 10:12-14.
3. The more sin, the more punishment.
   a. Punishment will be graded by the number of sins.
   b. Punishment will be further graded by the character of sin.
4. The tender Jesus will be the Judge who sentences people to Hell; John 5:22; Acts 10:42.

II. OBJECTIONS TO THE BIBLE DOCTRINE OF HELL.
1. To reject the Bible is to reject the atoning death of Christ.
   a. Rejectors reject the teaching that "Christ died for our sins"; I Cor. 15:3.
   b. Rejectors reject that Christ ". . . bare our sins in His own body on the tree"; I Peter 2:24.
2. To have forgiveness without atonement would be spiritual anarchy.
3. Misunderstood Scriptures.
   a. Revelation 22:11 is God's last sentence on the sinner.
   b. Another objection that is pressed is that the Bible teaches a Hell of literal fire and is therefore wrong. Yet it means literal fire when it says, "to be cast into Hell where their worm dieth not and the fire is not quenched."
4. Men sneer at the "fear motive."
   a. The objection is raised that they have never heard of Christ; John 1:19; Rom. 1:20.
   b. The objection concerning whether the unsaved will be lost without the gospel; Rom. 2:12, 14.
5. Scoffers, thinking that the Bible teaches Hell alike for all, accuse God of injustice.
   a. Romans 3:22 does not mean that all will suffer alike in Hell.
   b. The Lord Jesus said that there is a difference in the degrees of sin; John 19:11.

— Adapted from T. T. Martin

THE FAMILY RECORD
LUKE 16:19-31

INTRODUCTION: Jesus in this passage of Scripture which I have read to you from the sixteenth chapter of Luke gives a family record. He tells some very interesting things about an interesting family.

I. IT WAS A RICH FAMILY.
1. Jesus begins by telling us that this rich man had plenty of money. Oh, the worry that money brings!
2. It looks to me like the more money people get, the more wretched and unhappy they are.

II. IT WAS A BIG FAMILY.
1. There were six brothers — one dead and five living.
2. I love big families. The sweetest music the world has ever heard since the morning stars sang together is the laughter of little babies.

III. IT WAS A FAMILY VISITED BY DEATH.
1. Death is a wicked, cruel, conquering king.
2. Death's music is the cry of broken hearts, and his flowers are the faded garlands on coffin lids.
3. Death is the inevitable and Jesus Christ is the preparation. The wise man always makes preparation for the inevitable.

IV. IT WAS A FAMILY WITH ONE MEMBER IN HELL.
1. The rich man died and in Hell, he lifted up his eyes; Luke 16:22, 23.
2. It is not as bad to run an automobile over a little boy as it is for a parent to run the car of evil influence over a child and send his soul to Hell.

V. IT WAS A FAMILY WITH FIVE OTHERS ON THE WAY TO HELL.
1. The rich man wanted Abraham to send Lazarus back and ask his brothers not to come to Hell; Luke 16:27, 28.
2. Did you ever have a family reunion when they were not all there? It did not seem right, did it?
3. I have always thought that having the whole family in Heaven would make Heaven sweeter.

VI. IT WAS A FAMILY WHICH HAD EVERY NEEDED CHANCE TO BE SAVED.
1. They had the testimony of Moses and the prophets.
2. People today have a better chance for salvation than the rich man's family. People today have the gospel and the convicting power of the Holy Spirit.

— Bob Jones, Sr.

DIVINE PRINCIPLES OF EVANGELISM IN THE PRESENT AGE
ACTS 1:8; MATTHEW 28:19, 20

I. THIS EVANGELIZATION OF THE WORLD WAS THE UT-
TERMOST CONCERN WITH THE LORD JESUS WHEN HE
LEFT THIS EARTH TO RETURN TO THE FATHER.
  1. The commission of our Lord Jesus Christ to His disciples was
     given in a somewhat different form at least three times; Matt.
     28:18-20; Mark 16:15; Luke 24:46-48.
  2. The emphasis Christ laid upon evangelism reveals the deep con-
     cern of His own heart about it.
II. THE HOLY SPIRIT'S BEING GIVEN FOR THE PURPOSE OF
WORLD EVANGELIZATION, HE, UPON HIS COMING,
TOOK ABSOLUTE SUPERINTENDENCY OF THE WORK OF
THE LORD; Acts 2-5.
  1. The Holy Spirit directed Philip in his work; Acts 8:26, 29, 39.
  2. The Holy Spirit convinced Peter and the Jewish brethren with
     him that the Gentiles, too, could be saved and added to the
     Church; Acts 10:44-48; 11:17, 18.
  3. The Holy Spirit directed the Gentile Church at Antioch to sep-
     arate Barnabas and Saul for missionary work among the Gentiles;
     Acts 13:1-4.
  4. The Holy Spirit directed the first council at Jerusalem in their de-
     cision in reference to the relation of Gentile believers to the Law;
     Acts 15:28, 7-11.
  5. The Holy Spirit later restrained Paul, Silas, and Timothy from
     entering self-chosen fields of labor; Acts 16:6-11.
III. THE FIRST COUNCIL AT JERUSALEM RESULTED IN A
DECLARATION REVEALING GOD'S PROGRAM FOR THE
PRESENT AGE AND THE COMING DISPENSATION; Acts
15:14-17.
  1. God's present age purpose is "to take out" from among the Gen-
     tiles a "people for His Name"; Acts 15:14; Matt. 16:18; Rev. 5:9,
     10.
  2. The purpose of God for the coming dispensation is that the Lord
     Jesus will return to earth again, the Davidic Kingdom will be re-
     stored, Israel will be converted, and the nations brought to the
     Lord; Zech. 8:20-23; Matt. 28:18-20; 24:14.
IV. THE MACEDONIAN CALL PRESENTS THE SUPREME IL-
LUSTRATION OF MISSIONARY ENTERPRISE; Acts 16:9, 10.
  1. This call was a cry from the perishing.
  2. This call was the cry from a number of souls. "Help us."
  3. This call was a Divine call.
V. THE LORD'S PROGRAM CONCERNS EVERY CHRISTIAN.
  1. The Lord seeks the cooperation of all His people. They are viewed
     as co-workers together with Him; John 10:16; I Cor. 3:9; II Cor.
     6:1.
  2. The yielded Christian gladly yields to the call of the Lord.
  — Adapted from W. S. Hottel in *The Bible Expositor and Illuminator*

ON THE WAY TO THE DEATH CHAMBER
JOHN 3:18, 19

INTRODUCTION:

1. Not long since, I read the news story of a very noted criminal who was removed from all the other prisoners and taken over to the death chamber — a specially arranged room immediately adjoining the place of execution.

2. This noted criminal had been tried and convicted, of course, and the judge had called him before the bar and pronounced sentence upon him, that he should be electrocuted on a certain day. Following this formal sentence by the court, the sheriff had removed him from all the other prisoners and placed him in the death chamber. This news story made it clear that only a pardon or a commutation from the governor could save that man!

3. After reading this tragic story, I began to think about the great groups of men and women, all about us everywhere, who are already condemned under the laws of God and who are on their way to the death chamber of eternity, just as certain as there is a God in Heaven. Who are these people? John's Gospel lists them as follows:

I. THOSE WHO HEAR AND SEE AND REJECT THE LORD JESUS CHRIST; John 1:11, 12.

II. ALL WHO HAVE NOT BEEN BORN AGAIN; John 3:3-7.

III. ALL WHO DO NOT BELIEVE ON JESUS AS THE SON OF GOD; John 3:18, 19; 3:35, 36.

IV. ALL WHO DO NOT COME TO CHRIST FOR LIFE AND SALVATION; John 5:40; 6:35-37; 43, 44.

V. ALL WHO DO NOT RECEIVE JESUS AS THE BREAD OF LIFE; John 6:51-57.

VI. ALL WHO SEEK JESUS BUT SEEK HIM WHEN IT IS TOO LATE; John 7:33, 34; 8:21-24.

VII. PERSONS WHO REALLY BELIEVE IN JESUS BUT WHO LOVE THE PRAISE OF MEN MORE THAN THE PRAISE OF GOD; John 12:42, 43.

VIII. ALL MEMBERS OF THE CHURCH WHO HAVE ONLY A NOMINAL AND NOT A VITAL CONNECTION WITH CHRIST; John 15:16.

IX. THOSE WHO JOURNEY WITH JESUS AND OCCUPY HIGH POSITIONS IN HIS CHURCH BUT WHO HAVE NEVER BEEN CHANGED BY THE POWER OF GOD; John 6:70, 71; 17:12.

CONCLUSION: Unless these nine classes of people ask for and receive a pardon from God, two things are as certain as God:

1. In due time God will order His sheriff (death) to remove them to the death chamber.

2. God's sentence of condemnation will then be executed to the letter.

— E. P. Alldredge

PANOPLIED

EPHESIANS 6:11

INTRODUCTION: The title of this message is a word unfamiliar to our ears, yet it is one which embraces the substance of a vital truth and a great need. To be panoplied means to possess a protective covering, and in this instance, it means a full suit of armor. Because it is so important to be clad with "the whole armour of God," it would be well for us to consider each individual piece of it.

I. THE GIRDLE OF TRUTH.
  1. When God was preparing His people for the exodus from Egypt, He instructed them to eat the passover "with your loins girded," Exod. 12:13.
  2. Instructing His servants to be in readiness of His coming, the Saviour said, "Let your loins be girded about, . . ." Luke 12:35.

II. THE BREASTPLATE OF RIGHTEOUSNESS.
  1. We know the value of a breastplate as it shields the heart from the fierce blows of the enemy; Cf. I Cor. 1:30.
  2. In our standing before God, every believer is righteous, just as righteous as Jesus Himself; II Cor. 5:21.

III. THE SANDALS OF PEACE.
  1. We must take a firm hold upon the gospel as shoes for our feet, and go forth to declare the power of His saving grace; Eph. 2:14; Rom. 5:1.
  2. We need to be certain that we have the right message, otherwise we will be wearing a shoe which does not fit and we will be rendered unfit; John 14:27.

IV. THE SHIELD OF FAITH.
  1. Faith holds a vital place in the Christian experience; Heb. 11:6.
  2. The Lord Jesus is the object of faith and as we focus our attention upon Him and upon His Word "faith cometh."

V. THE HELMET OF SALVATION.
  1. It is that piece of equipment which protects the head and is most essential for the soldier.
  2. Christ is our salvation and only as we cast ourselves upon Him in utter dependence for daily deliverance will we be clad with the helmet; I Cor. 15:2.

VI. THE SWORD OF THE SPIRIT.
  1. It is not the fine scabbard that counts, it is the Word itself; Jer. 23:29.
  2. It is the means of the Word that sin is put to rout; Matt. 4; Luke 4.

— Adapted from R. S. Beal in *The Gospel Herald*

MISSING GOD'S LAST TRAIN FOR HEAVEN
JEREMIAH 8:20

INTRODUCTION: God's harvests pass away! Nothing in the world is so surely true that opportunities pass as of the matter of salvation.

I. THE HARVEST OF YOUTH PASSES.
1. Many Scriptures teach that youth is the time to be saved; Prov. 8:17; Eccl. 12:1; Matt. 19:14; 18:2, 3.
2. Experience proves, by actual canvass of multitudes, that nearly everybody ever saved is converted in youth.

II. THE HARVEST OF GOD'S SPECIAL DEALING PASSES.
1. The special dealing of wartime circumstances passes.
2. The special dealing of circumstances which accompanies accidents passes.
3. The special dealing of times of joy passes.
4. The special dealing of the approaching hour of death passes.

III. THE HARVEST WHEN THERE ARE REAPERS MAY PASS AWAY.
1. Lost sinner, there is hope for you to be saved if there are people who love you and pray for you and earnestly entreat you to repent and trust in Christ.
2. The boy who was not saved when he had a mother to warn him is not likely to be saved when he is beyond the reach of her pleadings.

IV. THE HARVEST OF THE HOLY SPIRIT'S CONVICTION AND PLEADING MAY PASS AWAY.
1. No one can be saved except when the Spirit of God calls him and convicts him of his sins; John 16:7-11.
2. Some day you may hear the last call from the Spirit of God when there is no more a moving of the Spirit, you are doomed; your harvest is ended; Gen. 6:3.

V. THE HARVEST AND OPPORTUNITY OF REVIVAL TIME PASS AWAY.
1. Most of the people ever saved are saved during revival seasons.
2. If you are unconverted and you go through a revival unconverted, then the closing of that special revival effort is the passing of a great slice of your opportunity to be saved.

VI. THE HARVEST OF LIFE ITSELF WILL CERTAINLY, PERHAPS SUDDENLY, PASS AWAY.
1. Nobody ever gets saved on the other side of death.
2. When death comes, then eternal doom comes for the unconverted sinner.

— Adapted from John R. Rice

CHRIST'S DEITY AND MAN'S SALVATION
JOHN 20:30, 31

INTRODUCTION: While purposing to treat this subject in such candor and fairness that even the demands of the critical mind may be met, we confess in advance our purpose is to bring our auditors to join with the consent that Jesus is the solitary Saviour.

To that end we propose three questions:

I. IS JESUS THE SON OF GOD?

1. History should speak to this subject. The historian has not yet been born who has, or could ignore the name of Jesus and yet command the respect of men.
2. The Scriptures, also, testify to His deity.
   a. The New Testament asserts it; Matt. 1:21.
   b. The worthy testimony of John records it; John 1:1, 14.
3. Christians also are credible witnesses to His deity; I John 1:1, 3.

II. IS JESUS THE SOLITARY SAVIOUR?

1. Is there no other person who can save?
   a. There was a day when the king put all the corn of Egypt into the hands of Joseph. Men must make their appeal to him or perish.
   b. Is it true of our Joseph that the stores of salvation are all in His hands? The Scriptures are strong; Acts 4:12.
2. There is no other way of salvation; John 14:6.

III. WHAT THEN IS ESSENTIAL FOR SALVATION?

1. To believe that Jesus is the Christ, the Son of God, is the first essential; John 20:30, 31.
2. Believe that eternal life is with Christ; I John 5:11.
   a. This proposition is plain.
   b. This declaration is decisive.
   c. This second step is absolutely essential.
3. Believe that He gives you salvation now; John 3:36.
   a. The men who have tested this declaration of the Scriptures have found salvation.
   b. The women who have brought to Him loyalty have come into the knowledge of life.
   c. The children who have sought Him have been received and saved.

— Adapted from W. B. Riley

47

THINGS NOT FOUND IN HELL
LUKE 16:19-31

INTRODUCTION: It is to be hoped that you are not going to Hell. The wicked are; Ps. 9:17. All men outside of Christ are wicked and lost; Rom. 3:10-12.

Some may say, "I don't care if I go to Hell or not." Let us see if it matters as we view what will not be in Hell. There will be:

I. NO REST IN HELL.
1. Condition of Hell. "Everlasting fire"; Matt. 18:8; Mark 9:48; Luke 16:24.
2. Continuance of Hell. No rest; Mark 9:46; Rev. 14:11; Matt. 25:46.

II. NO REVELATION IN HELL.
1. It is asserted. "Outer darkness"; Matt. 8:12; 22:13; 25:30.
2. It is argued, "How can Hell be a place of darkness with all its flame and fire."
3. It is answered. Hell can be a place of flame and fire to the senses and yet be utter darkness to the soul!
4. It is assured. The sinner is in darkness; Eph. 5:8. Christ is the Light; John 8:12. To reject Christ is to be in darkness "for ever"; Jude 13.

III. NO REDEMPTION IN HELL.
1. Beyond the help of the Passionate Christ; Job 36:18. Here we have redemption; Eph. 1:7; I Peter 1:18, 19. It will be too late after death.
2. Beyond hearing preaching about Christ; I Cor. 1:21; James 1:18.
3. Beyond help of praying to Christ. "Great gulf fixed!"
4. Beyond the pardon of Christ. No salvation in Hell; II Cor. 6:2; Heb. 9:27.

IV. NO RECESS IN HELL.
1. Here on earth suffering is temporary. The greatest sufferer can live in hope that some new cure can reach him soon and relieve him. Not so in Hell!
2. In Hell suffering will be timeless! On and on. No end! Matt. 25:46; II Thess. 1:9; Mark 9:43.

CONCLUSION: Between you and Hell there stands the cross of Christ. Come. Submit yourself to the crucified and risen Christ who is able to save you; I Cor. 15:3, 4; Heb. 7:25; Rom. 10:13. Be able to say, "Christ has delivered me from the wrath to come!" I Thess. 1:10. Until you do this you are lost and ready to drop into Hell at any moment.

— Adapted from Frank Beck